WHO'S HIDING... ∽in∽ Fairyland?

igloobooks

Who's hiding in Fairyland?

Annabelle and Tulip live in Fairyland with all of their magical friends. There are lots of things happening all over the land, from birthday parties to cloud mazes in the sky. Each picture in this book has all sorts of wonderful and interesting things for you to find. In fact, there are over 1000 things to be found in Fairyland! Annabelle and Tulip are in each picture, so you'll need to find them first. Then, each page has little pictures to show you what else you need to look for, from bumblebee space hoppers to rainbow crystals and everything in between! To get you started, can you spot Annabelle and Tulip playing in their magical garden?

Annabelle

Tulip

Can you find all of these items on the opposite page, too?

1 bird's nest

5 ladybirds

10 purple flowers

Toadstool Town

It's a very busy day in Toadstool Town. Annabelle and Tulip have decided to go shopping, can you spot them in the picture below?

Chestnuts

Now you've found Tulip and Annabelle, see if you can spot these things, too.

1 toadstool house

2 goblins

3 petal bikes

4 red doors

5 purple birds

6 poppies

7 pogo sticks

8 space hoppers

9 green presents

10 bags of chestnuts

20 blue snails

Flower Festival

There's a flower festival in Fairyland today. Can you find Fairies Tulip and Annabelle among all of their friends?

Now you've found Tulip and Annabelle, see if you can spot these things, too.

1 pink unicorn

2 squirrels

3 flutes

4 dancing mice

5 toffee apples

6 frogs

7 smiley red flowers

8 candy floss

9 yellow stars

10 purple sweeties

20 red hearts

Fairy Queen's Party

It's the Fairy Queen's birthday and everyone
in Fairyland is having a party. Can you
find fairies Annabelle and Tulip?

4 red balloons

5 chocolate puddings

6 lanterns

7 pink presents

Can you find all of these other items at the party, too?

1 birthday cake

2 petal thrones

3 blue butterflies

8 sandwiches

9 red roses

10 party hats

20 flower cookies

Crystal Cascades

It's a very hot day and all of the fairies are
cooling down at the Crystal Cascades. Can you
spot Fairy Annabelle and Fairy Tulip?

Now you've found Tulip and Annabelle, see if you can spot these things, too.

1 sweets shop

2 flamingos

3 lotion bottles

4 rubber rings

5 red swimsuits

6 pairs of green sunglasses

7 ice creams

8 floppy hats

9 yellow lizzards

10 starfish

20 pink pebbles

Rainbow Meadow

There's a rainbow stretching all across the meadow today. Can you spot Annabelle and Tulip among their fairy friends?

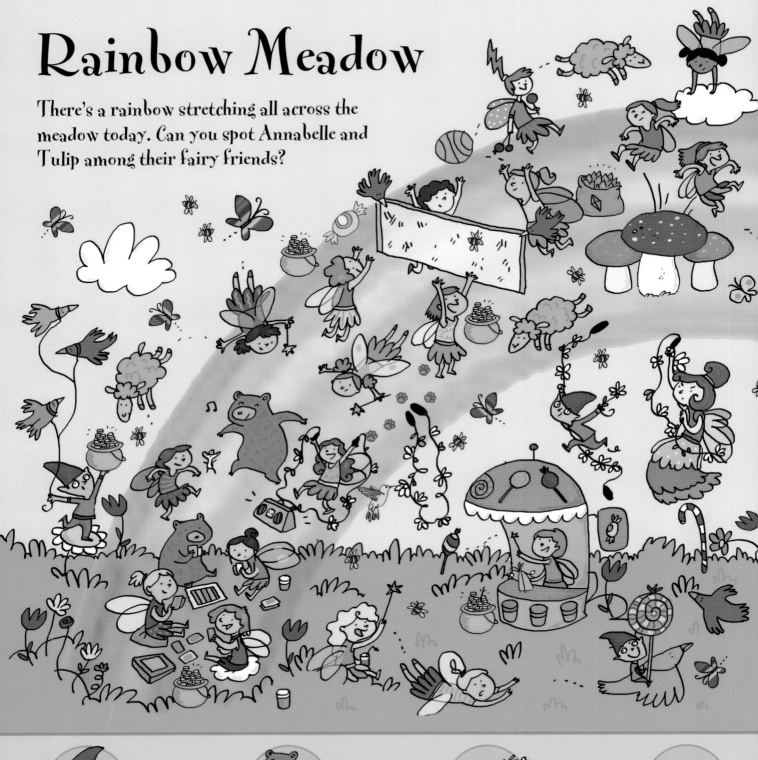

4 naughty pixies

5 brown bears

6 skipping ropes

7 pink sheep

1 volley ball

2 candy canes

3 bags of crystals

8 pots of gold

9 purple tulips

10 paw prints

20 bumble bees

Fairy Forest

The fairies are having lots of fun flying in and out of the trees in Firefly Forest. Can you spot Fairy Annabelle and Fairy Tulip among their friends?

Now you've found Tulip and Annabelle, see if you can spot these things, too.

1 camp fire

2 foxes

3 racoons

4 bunnies

5 wood sprites

6 pixies

 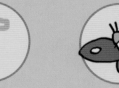

7 musical notes

8 purple moths

9 blue daisies

10 beetles

20 glow worms

Enchanted Lagoon

Tulip and Annabelle have come to the lagoon to cool and off and play with all of their friends. Can you find them?

4 purple bats

5 pink shells

6 lilypads

7 frogs

1 love heart boat

2 mermaids

3 turtles

8 rainbow fish

9 pond skater bugs

10 bubbles

20 fireflies

Treetop School

There is plenty going on at school today.
Can you spot fairies Annabelle and Tulip?

Can you find these other things
up in the treetop, too?

1 griffin

2 flower clocks

3 owls

4 leaf swings

5 purple bags

6 pencil cases

7 calculators
with wings

8 prefect badges

9 green books

10 pink leaves

20 ants

Fairy Show

Some of the fairies are putting on a show. Can you find Annabelle and Tulip among all of their fairy friends?

Fairy Show

4 pink microphones

5 blue spot lights

6 torches

7 cobwebs

Can you find all of these other items in the show, too?

1 tuba

2 purple curtains

3 violins

8 tubs of popcorn

9 bottles of water

10 purple slugs

20 roses

Cloud Maze

The fairies are playing up in the clouds.
Can you spot fairies Annabelle and
Tulip among their friends?

START

Can you find all of these other items in the show, too?

1 tuba

2 purple curtains

3 violins

8 tubs of popcorn

9 bottles of water

10 purple slugs

20 roses

Cloud Maze

The fairies are playing up in the clouds. Can you spot fairies Annabelle and Tulip among their friends?

START

Now you've found Tulip and Annabelle, see if you can spot these things, too.

1 flying trophy

2 flying horses

3 red hats

4 mice riding birds

5 scooters

6 green kites

7 pink clouds

8 blue flags

9 windmills

10 pairs of shorts

20 raindrops

FINISH

Well done, you've found everything in Fairyland! Now go back and see if you can find each of these extra items in every picture, too.

1 Fairy Queen

1 mushroom

1 yellow sweetie

1 centaur

1 green tulip

1 flag with a clover

1 daisy parasol

1 venus fly trap

1 swirly lollypop

1 fairy with spotty wings

1 humming bird

How closely were you looking? Do you know which picture each of these items were in?

10 cupcakes

10 blue diamonds

10 acorn lunchboxes

10 shooting stars

10 rainbow butterflies

10 radios

10 pairs of binoculars

10 millipedes

10 rose perfume

10 toy bunnies

CONTENTS

RBIRDS ANNUAL

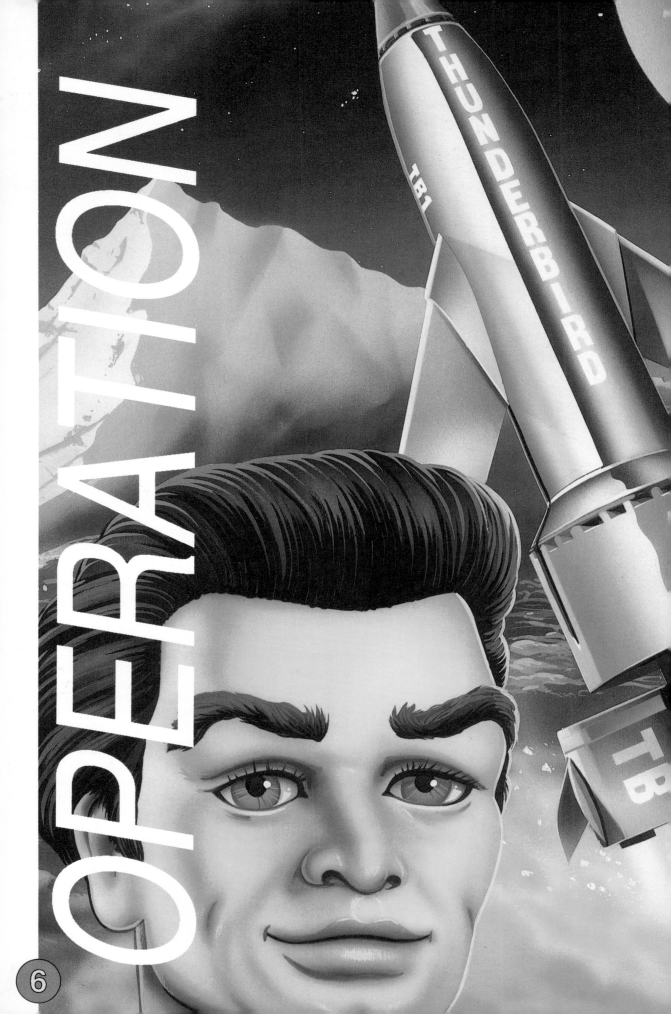

OPERATION

THUNDERBIRD
TB1
TB

6

£4.75

THUND

Published by
Grandreams Limited
Jadwin House
205-211 Kentish Town Road
London NW5 2JU

Printed in Italy

THUNDERBIRDS MISSION

COMPUTER CONTROLLED from the American mainland, target ship Ocean Trader sailed smoothly across the wide loneliness of the central Pacific Ocean.

Packed with electronics, the old freighter was making her last voyage, steaming towards the centre of a red circle marked on the charts spread out in the control command of Missile Research centre Western X, somewhere north of San Francisco.

Chief controller Irving Ableman spoke clearly into the microphone on his desk. "Ocean Trader entering red zone now. Check systems."

Admiral Wallace Johnson sat by the central console and watched green lights flick on and off in succession. He looked at his watch. "Fire missile," he said evenly, and his thumb came down on a polished aluminium button.

Out on the launch pad, a Masterstrike rocket began its lift-off, a ten-megaton tritherium warhead at its nose, and Admiral Johnson sat back and wiped his perspiring brow.

"There she goes," he said with satisfaction. "Computers do the rest....all we have to do is wait."

On Tracy Island, far to the south of the target zone, the International Rescue team were just as interested in this latest research shot as the rest of the world. Brains, the scientist, was already checking the detector-recording apparatus in his laboratory.

"This - er - really is an ambitious one," he stammered to Jeff Tracy. "The ultimate in computer controlled guidance systems. It s-seems they're putting the Masterstrike into a s-single orbit of the earth. There's a homing device in the target ship. The device has a greater range than anything tried before. Once the pre-determined trigger is operated, the guidance system will lock onto the homer and b-bring the rocket right down on top of the ship. Then p-pow!"

"You mean that missile will be flying around the earth with no ground control?" Jeff asked with a frown.

"N-No, Mr Tracy," replied Brains. "Everything is linked to Research Centre Western X. They have complete electronic influence on the entire project."

"Beats me why they have to continue to develop bigger and more efficient weapons," mumbled Jeff. "If they spent as much money on peaceful scientific pursuits, the world would be a better place."

If Jeff had been aware of the problem that was about to develop, he would have been even more upset about the project. Jeff could not have known, and the technicians at Missile Research Centre Western X would not have dreamed it - something was about to happen that would bring their carefully laid plans towards impending disaster, something as simple as the brakes of a petroleum truck!

IT HAPPENED on the long hill that led up from the North California main power station, where the double-trailer fuel tanker was parked. The driver was having a coffee in a roadside transport pull-up. Why the main connector pipe of the lorry's air brakes chose that precise moment to spring a fault, only fate could say. One minute the big tanker's wheels were locked, the next, they were turning...and four hundred gallons of petrol went careering backwards down the hill.

The lorry smashed through the power station's perimeter wire and jack-knifed. The trailer swung round and sheared its way through the outer wall of the power station and burst into flames. Snaking power cables fell in all directions, blasting blue sparks in a succession of shattering flashes...and then the main generators burst like bombs.

Chief Controller Irving Ableman was on the point of announcing the near completion of the Masterstrike rocket's first and only orbit, when everything suddenly went dead. Every instrument, every control, every light went out. In the total darkness, there was only the confusion of terrifying panic!

Telephones, radio...all communication systems were useless. Target ship Ocean Trader cut from its control, and with only its self-contained apparatus working, continued on unchecked towards the edge of the red circle safety zone. And Masterstrike, under its pre-set course computers was completely divorced from all human control.

Admiral Johnson's voice was high-pitched with fear. "Ocean Trader's on a locked course...its homer is going to click on and pull down that bomb ...and we can only guess where the ship's going to be when it strikes!"

CONTINUED ON PAGE 15

8

LAUNCH SEQUENCE
THUNDERBIRD 1

When a call for help is received, the reconnaissance craft Thunderbird 1 is the first to be launched Pilot Scott Tracy grips light brackets in the lounge (panel 1), triggering a revolving door and floor which spins him into TB1's hangar under the house. The wall turns back into place as Scott steps forward on to the gantry (panel 2), which feeds forward to the entry hatch in TB1 (panel 3).

Having quickly changed into uniform, Scott sits at the controls of TB1 carrying out pre-flight checks as the craft is carried down to the Launch Bay on a computer-controlled trolley.

TB1 emerges from the tunnel to the Launch Bay located under the swimming pool in front of the house. The trolley comes to a halt over the Exhaust Blast Pit, and a brief automated countdown begins.

The swimming pool, concealing the entrance to the Launch Bay, slides back under the patio.

Thunderbird 1 blasts off. When returning to base, the launch procedure is reversed, with re-entry under the control of a computer guidance system.

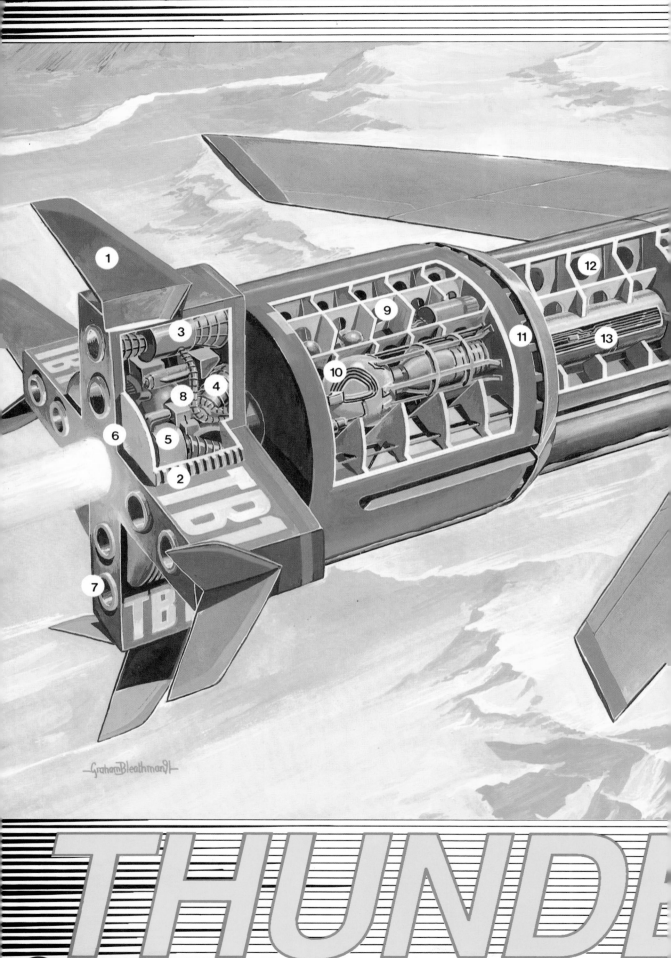

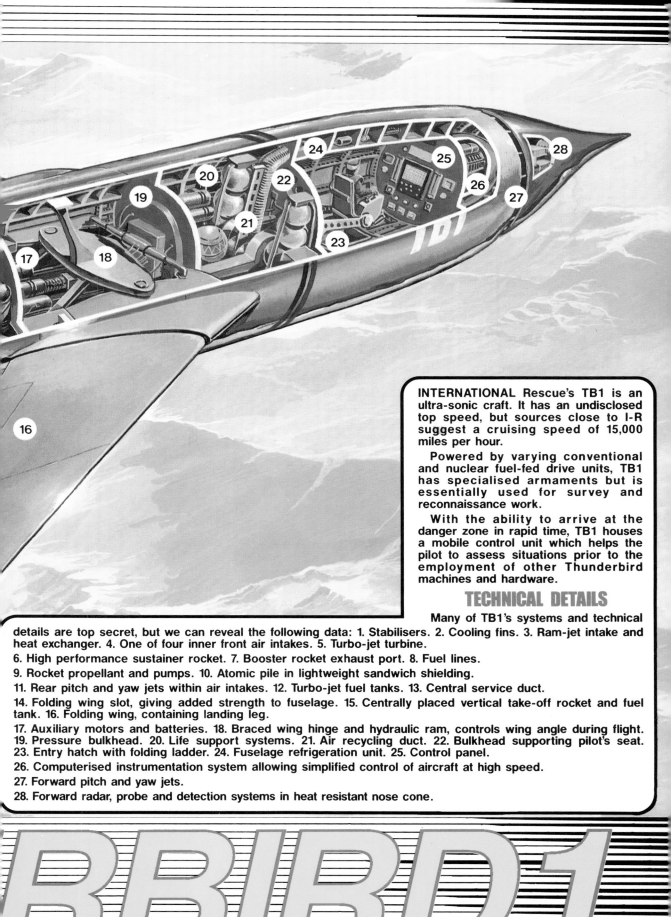

INTERNATIONAL Rescue's TB1 is an ultra-sonic craft. It has an undisclosed top speed, but sources close to I-R suggest a cruising speed of 15,000 miles per hour.

Powered by varying conventional and nuclear fuel-fed drive units, TB1 has specialised armaments but is essentially used for survey and reconnaissance work.

With the ability to arrive at the danger zone in rapid time, TB1 houses a mobile control unit which helps the pilot to assess situations prior to the employment of other Thunderbird machines and hardware.

TECHNICAL DETAILS

Many of TB1's systems and technical details are top secret, but we can reveal the following data: 1. Stabilisers. 2. Cooling fins. 3. Ram-jet intake and heat exchanger. 4. One of four inner front air intakes. 5. Turbo-jet turbine.

6. High performance sustainer rocket. 7. Booster rocket exhaust port. 8. Fuel lines.

9. Rocket propellant and pumps. 10. Atomic pile in lightweight sandwich shielding.

11. Rear pitch and yaw jets within air intakes. 12. Turbo-jet fuel tanks. 13. Central service duct.

14. Folding wing slot, giving added strength to fuselage. 15. Centrally placed vertical take-off rocket and fuel tank. 16. Folding wing, containing landing leg.

17. Auxiliary motors and batteries. 18. Braced wing hinge and hydraulic ram, controls wing angle during flight. 19. Pressure bulkhead. 20. Life support systems. 21. Air recycling duct. 22. Bulkhead supporting pilot's seat. 23. Entry hatch with folding ladder. 24. Fuselage refrigeration unit. 25. Control panel.

26. Computerised instrumentation system allowing simplified control of aircraft at high speed.

27. Forward pitch and yaw jets.

28. Forward radar, probe and detection systems in heat resistant nose cone.

RBIRD1

THUNDERBIRDS

FOR OVER 200 YEARS, HUALALAI HAS BEEN ASLEEP. THEN, EARLY ONE MORNING, THE VOLCANO AWAKES... IN AN ANGRY MOOD...

THE VOLCANO ON HUALALAI ERUPTS WITH FIRE AND BURNING ASH... AND FROM THE DEEP CRATER, SCALDING LAVA OOZES FORTH...

THE VILLAGE OF KALAOKA IS THREATENED...THROUGH THE ASH AND SMOKE, HELICOPTERS START TO AIRLIFT THE VILLAGERS TO SAFETY...

KEEP THE VILLAGERS IN THEIR HOMES. THIS ASH WILL CHOKE THEM. CONDITIONS ARE GETTING WORSE. WE WON'T BE ABLE TO FLY IN MANY MORE TIMES...

THE VISIBILITY FALLS TO ZERO...

IT'S NO GOOD. THAT WAS THE LAST COPTER MISSION WE CAN RISK.

HOW CAN WE RESCUE THESE PEOPLE...? THE LAVA FLOW IS HEADING THIS WAY FAST...

THEN AN OFFICIAL IN WASHINGTON HAS AN IDEA...

CALLING INTERNATIONAL RESCUE – THIS IS THE STATE DEPARTMENT, COLONEL RUTHIN HERE. WE NEED YOUR HELP...

IN THUNDERBIRD 5 JOHN TRACY RECEIVES A CALL...

GO AHEAD, COLONEL...

THE VILLAGERS OF KALAOKA ARE TRAPPED...

IN HIS PACIFIC ISLAND HOME JEFF TRACY, HEAD OF INTERNATIONAL RESCUE, TALKS TO HIS SON JOHN...

OKAY, JOHN, WE'VE BEEN KEEPING OUR EYES ON THE SITUATION...

SCOTT, VIRGIL – LAUNCH THUNDERBIRDS 1 AND 2... YOU'D BETTER GO WITH VIRGIL, BRAINS...

Y–YES, MR. TRACY. WE'LL NEED THE MOLE AND THE FIREFLY.

SOON SCOTT IS BLASTING OFF IN THUNDERBIRD 1...

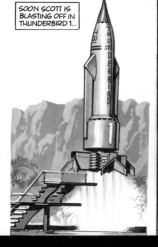

IN THUNDERBIRD 2, VIRGIL SELECTS THE REQUIRED POD.

THUNDERBIRDS ACTION IS ALWAYS HOT NEWS. THE HOOD, A SINISTER FIGURE, IS ESPECIALLY INTERESTED.

ONCE I HAVE INTERNATIONAL RESCUE'S SECRETS, THERE ARE POWERS WHO WILL PAY ME ME A FORTUNE... AND THOSE SECRETS WILL BE MINE!

FIRE MOUNTAIN

HUALALAI, A VOLCANO ON THE ISLAND OF HAWAII, HAS ERUPTED. SMOKE AND ASH HALT RESCUE ATTEMPTS AND A LAVA FLOW THREATENS THE VILLAGE OF KALAOKA. THUNDERBIRDS 1 AND 2 ARE LAUNCHED TO HELP...

THUNDERBIRD 1 TO THUNDERBIRD 2. IT SURE LOOKS BAD DOWN THERE, VIRGIL.

WE'LL LAND AS CLOSE AS WE CAN. BRAINS SAYS FIREFLY WILL WITHSTAND THE HEAT...

I'LL CHECK THINGS OUT AT THE VILLAGE...

IT SHOULD BE ALL RIGHT, VIRGIL. YOU CAN USE THE WATER JETS TO KEEP THE VISOR CLEAR OF ASH.

THUNDERBIRD 2 IS RAISED TO ALLOW THE POD DOOR TO OPEN...

WHILE SCOTT HEADS FOR KALAOKA, VIRGIL REACHES THE RIM OF THE CRATER...

FIREFLY TO THUNDERBIRD 1. IT'S A REAL BOILER! I JUST HOPE THE PLAN WORKS...

IN THE THUNDERBIRD 2 LABORATORY, BRAINS MAKES FINAL CALCULATIONS FROM THE REPORT TRANSMITTED BY VIRGIL...

Y-YES... THAT SHOULD DO IT. THE MOLE NEEDS TO BE OVER BY POINT FIVE DEGREES.

IN THE MEANTIME, IN HIS TEMPLE IN A MALAYSIAN JUNGLE, THE HOOD CASTS HIS HYPNOTIC SPELL...

KYRANO, MY BROTHER...YOU WILL HELP ME TO GET INTO THE HOUSE ON TRACY ISLAND. YOU ARE FEELING UNWELL...

JEFF TRACY'S FAITHFUL MANSERVANT IS WITH HIS DAUGHTER TIN TIN...

WHAT IS IT, FATHER...?

AAAGH!

A DOCTOR IS CALLED BUT THE ILLNESS IS A MYSTERY.

ALL HIS FUNCTIONS ARE NORMAL, BUT HE SEEMS TO BE IN DEEP SHOCK...

JEFF AND TIN TIN AGREE NOT TO WORRY THE BOYS ABOUT KYRANO'S CONDITION...

THEY HAVE ENOUGH PROBLEMS WITH THAT VOLCANO.

THANKS, DOC. WE'LL CALL YOU IF THERE'S ANY CHANGE.

WE HAVEN'T MUCH TIME, VIRGIL...

I KNOW, SCOTT. WE'LL BE READY FOR THE MOLE SOON. YOU'D BETTER GET UP HERE...

CONTINUED ON PAGE 20

13

COLOURING PAGE

14

CONTINUED FROM PAGE 8

›› OPERATION MASTERSTRIKE

ON CONSTANT, watchful orbit above the earth, space station Thunderbird 5 had been tuned to the transmissions from Missile Research Centre Western X. Now the transmission had suddenly gone dead, and John Tracy wanted to know why.

It didn't take the young man from International Rescue long to flick over the directional switches and pick up the frantic scramble of messages between Northern California fire departments. And once John Tracy knew that the main power station had been blasted to a halt, he was soon able to fit the pieces of the jigsaw together and relay what he knew to headquarters on Tracy Island.

It was Brains who supplied the missing pieces of the puzzle, to reach the same desperate conclusion as Admiral Johnson.

Jeff Tracy's face was grimly serious. "Where is Ocean Trader going to be when the rocket makes its dive, Brains?"

"Th-that's just it, M-Mr Tracy," stuttered Brains. "Ocean Trader's heading this way...and I - eh estimate it will have reached within four miles of Tracy Island!"

Alan, Virgil and Scott Tracy had come into the lounge. Now they shifted their feet, nervously, as their father sprang upright from his desk. "We have to turn that ship," barked Jeff. "Can you take over control, Brains?"

"Impossible, Mr Tracy", shrugged the scientist. "Only the people at the research station know the wavelengths and frequencies - and we can't reach them!"

Jeff Tracy swung round on Scott. "Get Thunderbird into the air immediately," he snapped. "Virgil, you'd better follow with Brains in

Thunderbird 2. You'll have to play it by ear...but first thing is to get aboard Ocean Trader - and quickly!"

THREE - WAY radio contact was in full and open operation as Thunderbird 1 hurtled at low level across the blue mirror of the Pacific. Scott Tracy could hear Brains from Thunderbird 2, twenty minutes behind him.

"Have you s-sighted the ship yet, Scott? We're running out of time! By my calculations, the M - asterstrike is approaching d of its orbit...we've got e than ten minutes!"

ott gripped the controls aft until his knuckles white. "How long after that Brains? How long before Masterstrike comes down?"

A brief silence. Then Brains again. "Fifteen minutes. The rocket's in high orbit."

Suddenly, Scott yelled with triumph, "There she is! Ocean Trader...dead ahead!"

Scott slammed down the switch that fired the down-thruster rockets beneath Thunderbird 1, and brutally hauled the craft into a metal-wrenching turn. Quietly, menacingly, the target ship steered its relentless course beneath him.

"Five minutes!" He licked his lips. "Brains - is there any point in sinking the ship?"

Brains groaned aloud.

"Useless, Scott. The homer would still work. And there's a coral shelf down there. The explosion might not hit Tracy Island, but the tidal wave..."

"I'm going to put Thunderbird down on her deck," said Scott. "Join me as soon as you can...I'll need you to identify the equipment, Brains!"

SCOTT STOOD on the forepart of the deck of Ocean Trader. His left hand was held level with his face. His eyes flickered constantly from the dial of his watch to the huge bulk of Thunderbird 2 which hovered above. Slowly the great craft dropped down lower and lower.

Now a steel ladder was being lowered, and Brains was scrambling down it, dropping the last six feet to the deck.

"One minute and fifty seconds," yelled Scott. "We have to find that homer!"

Brains rushed past him and climbed down the main companion way towards the old freighter's bridge where the computer control panel had been installed.

Scott was familiar with computers: all the Thunderbirds craft were equipped with the latest in technology, but he would not have known where to start to disarm the homing device.

Then again, Brains was a genius. He took precious seconds just studying the read-outs and cursors that flashed across the monitor screens before him.

Scott, almost leaping in the air with frustration, glanced at his watch and willed Brains to hurry. Then the little scientist operated some keys, turned some switches and pressed some buttons. But even as he activated the last control, there was a shrill buzzing sound screaming from the

CONTINUED ON PAGE 32

16

LAUNCH SEQUENCE
THUNDERBIRD 2

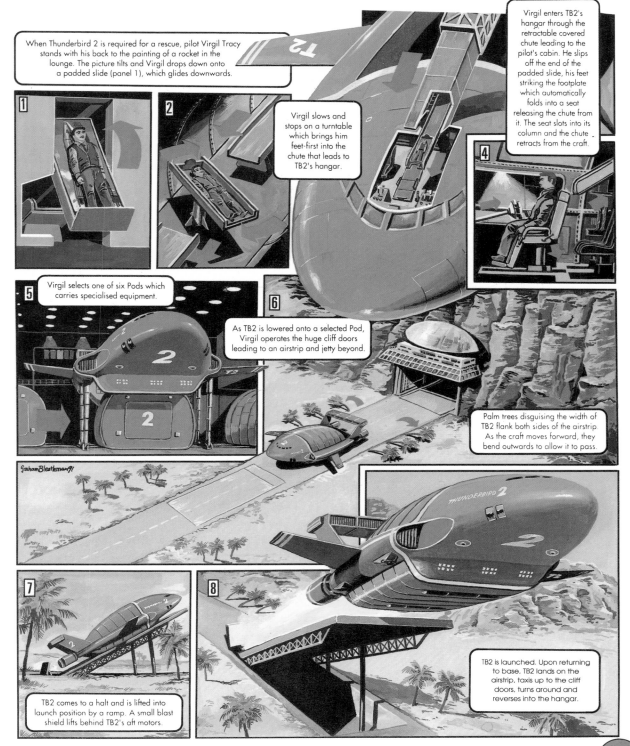

When Thunderbird 2 is required for a rescue, pilot Virgil Tracy stands with his back to the painting of a rocket in the lounge. The picture tilts and Virgil drops down onto a padded slide (panel 1), which glides downwards.

Virgil enters TB2's hangar through the retractable covered chute leading to the pilot's cabin. He slips off the end of the padded slide, his feet striking the footplate which automatically folds into a seat releasing the chute from it. The seat slots into its column and the chute retracts from the craft.

1

2

Virgil slows and stops on a turntable which brings him feet-first into the chute that leads to TB2's hangar.

4

5 Virgil selects one of six Pods which carries specialised equipment.

6

As TB2 is lowered onto a selected Pod, Virgil operates the huge cliff doors leading to an airstrip and jetty beyond.

Palm trees disguising the width of TB2 flank both sides of the airstrip. As the craft moves forward, they bend outwards to allow it to pass.

Graham Bleathman 91

THUNDERBIRD 2

7

8

TB2 is launched. Upon returning to base, TB2 lands on the airstrip, taxis up to the cliff doors, turns around and reverses into the hangar.

TB2 comes to a halt and is lifted into launch position by a ramp. A small blast shield lifts behind TB2's aft motors.

RENOWNED for its power and strength, Thunderbirds 2 is constructed of an alloy developed by Hiram Heckenbacker, known to the I-R team as Brains. With interchangeable pods, TB2 carries vital heavy engineering and life-saving equipment at speed to the danger zone. While precise details are classified, a cruising speed of 2,000mph at an altitude of 60,000 feet has been recorded.

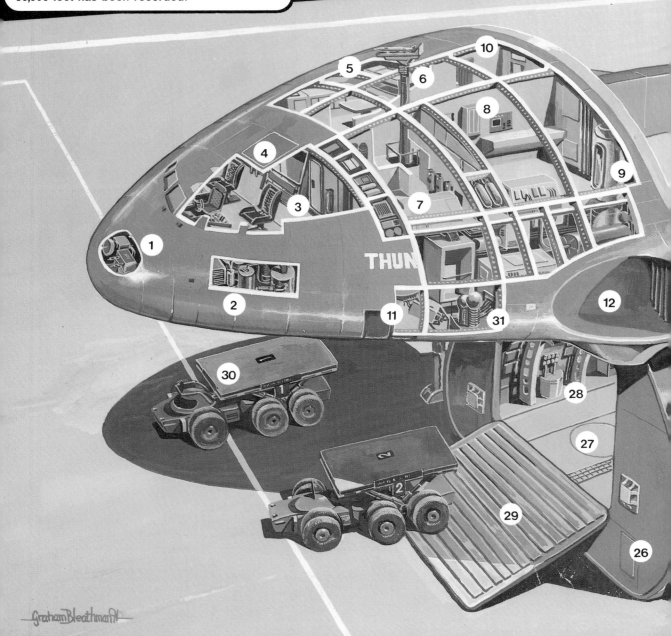

Graham Bleathman

TECHNICAL DATA

1. Forward radar and detection unit.
2. Fuselage refrigeration and air recycling unit.
3. Pilot's cabin.
4. Chute entry hatch.
5. Living accommodation.
6. Missile launcher.
7. Hand-held rescue equipment store.
8. Laboratory.
9. Lift to floor level pod door.
10. Entry hatch to pod overhead gallery.
11. Observation window with TV scanners.
12. Ramjet air intake.
13. Hydraulic landing gear in airflow fairing.
14. Primary heat exchanger.
15. Split duct around aft landing leg hydraulics.
16. Re-heat secondary heat exchanger.
17. Magnetic bolts to secure pod in flight.
18. Starboard vertical take-off rocket.
19. Rocket fuel tanks and pumps.
20. Atomic pile in lightweight shielding supplies heat to jet exchanges and turbo electrical generators.
21. Cruising speed turbo jets.
22. Ram-air turbine providing emergency electrical power.
23. Booster rocket for ramp launch.
24. Remote-controlled elevator car in pod.
25. Inner stressed wall providing strength to pod's lightweight fuselage.
26. Door giving access to lift when in flight.
27. Equipment turntable.
28. Pod vehicle maintenance equipment.
29. Ramp doubles as pod door.
30. Master elevator car.
31. Forward vertical take-off rocket, next to lift.

CONTINUED FROM PAGE 13

A VOLCANO ON THE ISLAND OF HAWAII HAS ERUPTED. INTERNATIONAL RESCUE IS TRYING TO DIVERT THE LAVA FLOW THAT THREATENS THE VILLAGE OF KALAOKA...

FIREFLY TO MOLE, ARE YOU READY, SCOTT?

NEXT SECOND...

I'VE LOCKED IN ON THE CO-ORDINATES. KEEP A CHECK ON THE TRACKING SCREEN, BRAINS.

FAB, SCOTT. IF YOU MAINTAIN THE ANGLE WE CALCULATED YOU SHOULD BE FINE.

AS SCOTT DIRECTS THE MOLE TOWARDS THE VOLCANO'S DEPTHS, ON TRACY ISLAND...

I MUST SEE MY BROTHER! I MUST SEE MY BROTHER!

HE KEEPS CALLING FOR MY UNCLE, MR. TRACY.

WE CAN'T HAVE ANYONE ON THE ISLAND UNTIL THIS RESCUE MISSION IS OVER...

THE MOLE BURROWS DOWN AT A STEADY ANGLE...

I'M ABOUT AS FAR AS I CAN GO WITHOUT PENETRATING THE INSIDE OF THE VOLCANO...

THAT'S FAR ENOUGH, SCOTT. WITHDRAW AND LET VIRGIL TAKE OVER IN FIREFLY.

I'LL FIRE WHEN YOU'RE CLEAR, SCOTT.

THE MOLE BACKS AWAY AND FIREFLY LINES UP WITH THE NEWLY CREATED TUNNEL. THEN...

A POWERFUL NITROGLYCERINE SHELL BLASTS THE LAST INCHES OF ROCKS AT THE END OF THE TUNNEL DUG BY THE MOLE...

THE MOLTEN LAVA FINDS A NEW COURSE...

UNDER EXTREME PRESSURE, THE RELEASED LAVA GUSHES TO THE SURFACE...

FIREFLY IS NOT RESPONDING TO THE CONTROLS. THE LAVA IS PULLING ME ROUND...!

THUNDERBIRDS 1 AND 2 RETURN FROM A RESCUE MISSION TO SAVE VILLAGERS FROM A HAWAIIAN VOLCANIC ERUPTION. THEY APPROACH TRACY ISLAND...

THUNDERBIRD 1 TO BASE, LANDING APPROACH NOW.

FAB, SCOTT. AS SOON AS YOU LAND COME STRAIGHT TO THE LOUNGE. WE'RE GOING TO HAVE A GUEST.

SCOTT, VIRGIL AND BRAINS JOIN THE FAMILY.

KYRANO HAS BEEN CALLING FOR HIS STEP-BROTHER. I'VE DECIDED HE CAN PAY US A VISIT IF IT WILL HELP TIN TIN'S FATHER RECOVER.

WHO IS THIS GUY, FATHER?

I KNOW VERY LITTLE ABOUT MY UNCLE. IT SEEMS HE IS CALLED MR. HOOD.

WELL, OPERATION COVER UP MUST BE MAINTAINED AT ALL TIMES. WE CAN'T RISK HIM STUMBLING ON OUR SECRETS.

AN HOUR LATER, THE HOOD'S AIRCRAFT ARRIVES.

MR. HOOD IS GREETED BY THE FAMILY AND ASKS TO BE ALONE WITH KYRANO...

LISTEN TO ME, KYRANO... YOU MUST HELP ME SEE THE THUNDERBIRD MACHINES. I NEED A PLAN OF THE HOUSE...

MY BROTHER IS WEAK... HE RESISTS MY POWER. I WILL HAVE TO SEARCH ALONE.

SCOTT TRACY HAS THE FEELING THAT HE HAS SEEN THE STRANGE VISITOR BEFORE...

WHERE'S HE OFF TO? THE LOUNGE IS IN THE OTHER DIRECTION. I'M SURE THIS GUY IS A PHONEY!

CAN I HELP YOU, MR. HOOD. THE REST OF THE FAMILY ARE THIS WAY. DON'T I KNOW YOU FROM SOMEWHERE?

IT IS MY RESEMBLANCE TO MY BROTHER, THAT'S ALL...

LATER THAT DAY, THERE IS A TELEPHONE CALL FOR JEFF...

OH, HI, PENELOPE. IT'S GOOD TO HEAR YOU. YES, I HOPE TO SEE YOU IN LONDON LATER THIS MONTH...

THE HOOD TAKES SPECIAL NOTE OF THE INNOCENT CONVERSATION. LATER, IN HIS BEDROOM...

PENELOPE... I HAD SOME TROUBLE WITH LADY PENELOPE IN ENGLAND...

I'M SURE SHE'S CONNECTED WITH INTERNATIONAL RESCUE. SHE SHOULD NOT BE TOO DIFFICULT TO TRACE...

THE HOOD, ONE OF THE WORLD'S BIGGEST VILLAINS, HAS MANAGED TO BECOME A HOUSE GUEST AT TRACY ISLAND. HE OVERHEARS JEFF TRACY TALKING TO LADY PENELOPE ON THE TELEPHONE. THE NEXT DAY...

I WILL TRACE LADY PENELOPE. BUT BEFORE I LEAVE I'LL SEE WHAT ELSE I CAN LEARN.

THE HOOD'S SNOOPING DOES NOT GO UNNOTICED.

I'M SURE WE'VE RUN UP AGAINST THIS CHARACTER BEFORE, FATHER.

OKAY, SCOTT. GUESS MR. HOOD HAS OUTSTAYED HIS WELCOME. I DON'T LIKE THE WAY HE PROWLS AROUND.

THE HOOD IS ASKED TO LEAVE...

ONCE THE HOOD HAS GONE, KYRANO SEEMS TO RECOVER COMPLETELY...

IT'S GOOD TO HAVE YOU UP AND ABOUT AGAIN, KYRANO.

BUT YOU MUST TAKE THINGS GENTLY, FATHER. YOU'VE BEEN VERY POORLY...

WHILE AT THE ISLAND, THE HOOD HAS HAD A CHANCE TO MIMIC JEFF TRACY'S VOICE. A WEEK LATER, AT THE STATELY HOME OF LADY PENELOPE...

IS FAB 1 READY, PARKER? IT SEEMS THERE IS SOME TROUBLE AT THE CHANNEL TUNNEL...

YUS, M'LADY. I 'EARD THERE 'AD BEEN A CAVE-IN...

IT IS UNLIKELY INTERNATIONAL RESCUE WILL BE REQUIRED, BUT MR. TRACY WANTS US GIVE HIM A FIRST-HAND REPORT.

A BATTERED TRUCK PULLS ALONGSIDE FAB 1.

THE TRUCK COMES VERY CLOSE...

OY, MATE... MOVE OVER!

NEXT SECOND...

AS PARKER COLLAPSES, THE TRUCK SWINGS INTO FAB 1...

CONTINUED ON PAGE 36 ▶ 23

FIREFLASH FLAME-OUT!

Thunderbird 5 receives an urgent call. A Fireflash aircraft has experienced a failed engine - a flame-out ! Starting at Tracy Island, you must follow the instructions as you progress around the game board to reach the Danger Zone.

This game can be played by any number of players. Why not challenge your friends?

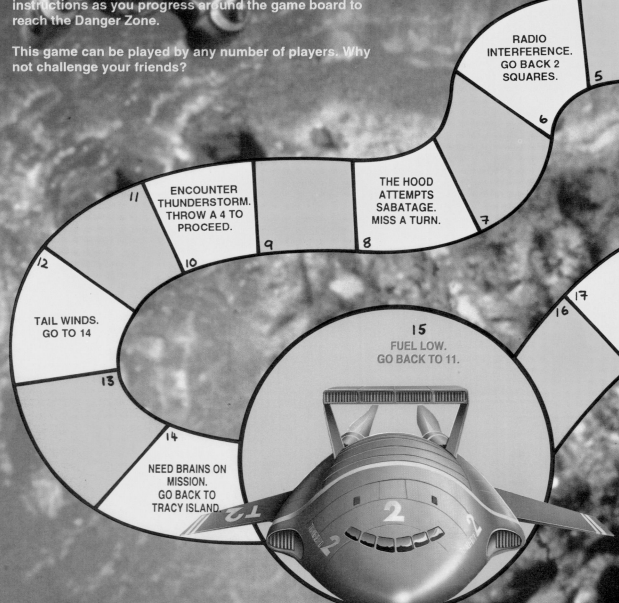

RADIO INTERFERENCE. GO BACK 2 SQUARES.

5

6

11

ENCOUNTER THUNDERSTORM. THROW A 4 TO PROCEED.

THE HOOD ATTEMPTS SABATAGE. MISS A TURN.

9

8

7

12

10

TAIL WINDS. GO TO 14

15
FUEL LOW.
GO BACK TO 11.

17

16

13

14

NEED BRAINS ON MISSION. GO BACK TO TRACY ISLAND.

FORGET VITAL RESCUE EQUIPMENT. GO BACK TO TRACY ISLAND

2

1

3

4
USE NEW BOOSTER ROCKET. GO TO 11

21

20
MALFUNCTION IN ELEVATOR CARS. MISS A TURN.

22

23

19

THROW A 6 TO REACH DANGER ZONE.

WORD SEARCH

T	R	A	C	Y	V	R	Y	Y	T	I	N
T	H	O	O	D	E	L	D	V	G	K	T
E	V	U	G	G	F	A	A	Z	Y	V	I
J	O	H	N	E	L	L	V	R	O	I	N
E	V	A	R	D	G	A	A	E	V	N	G
F	D	I	V	P	E	N	E	L	O	P	E
F	F	A	B	G	O	R	D	O	N	L	I
I	S	L	A	N	D	V	B	M	V	G	T
N	G	R	A	N	D	M	A	I	R	I	T
T	V	I	R	E	U	C	S	E	R	V	O
E	B	R	A	I	N	S	V	I	R	D	C
R	N	A	T	I	O	N	A	L	G	I	S

Brains has set this special test to see how observant you are. The following words are hidden in the grid. The words may appear straight, backwards, diagonally or even going around corners.

Find these words listed on the right:

An important element of the Thunderbirds set up is missing. Who or what is it? Solution on page 45.

~~HOOD~~	ISLAND
THUNDERBIRDS	FIREFLY
JEFF	LADY
ALAN	~~PENELOPE~~
~~SCOTT~~	KYRANO
~~JOHN~~	~~GRANDMA~~
~~GORDON~~	TIN TIN
MOLE	BRAINS
~~VIRGIL~~	~~FAB~~
RESCUE	DANGER
	ZONE

LAUNCH SEQUENCE
THUNDERBIRD 3

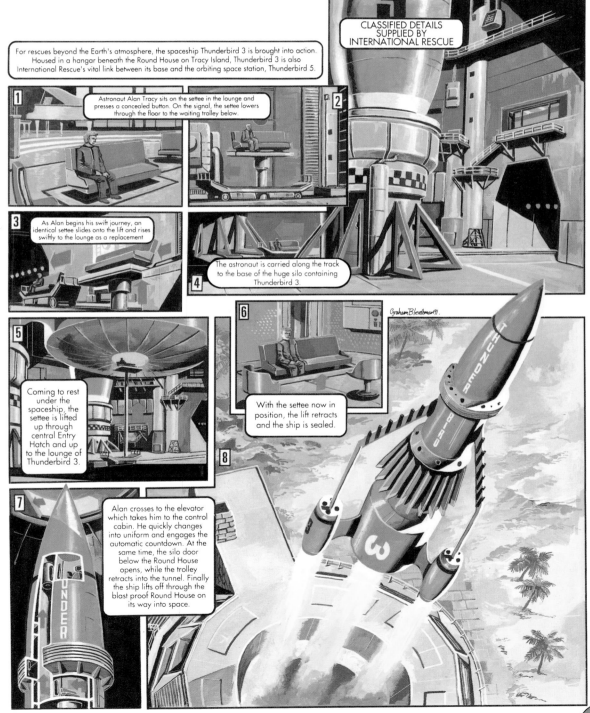

CLASSIFIED DETAILS
SUPPLIED BY
INTERNATIONAL RESCUE

For rescues beyond the Earth's atmosphere, the spaceship Thunderbird 3 is brought into action. Housed in a hangar beneath the Round House on Tracy Island, Thunderbird 3 is also International Rescue's vital link between its base and the orbiting space station, Thunderbird 5.

1 Astronaut Alan Tracy sits on the settee in the lounge and presses a concealed button. On the signal, the settee lowers through the floor to the waiting trolley below.

3 As Alan begins his swift journey, an identical settee slides onto the lift and rises swiftly to the lounge as a replacement

4 The astronaut is carried along the track to the base of the huge silo containing Thunderbird 3.

5 Coming to rest under the spaceship, the settee is lifted up through central Entry Hatch and up to the lounge of Thunderbird 3.

6 With the settee now in position, the lift retracts and the ship is sealed.

7 Alan crosses to the elevator which takes him to the control cabin. He quickly changes into uniform and engages the automatic countdown. At the same time, the silo door below the Round House opens, while the trolley retracts into the tunnel. Finally the ship lifts off through the blast proof Round House on its way into space.

Graham Bleathman 91.

THUNDERB

3

ALAN Tracy pilots TB3. Scott, and sometimes Brains and Tin Tin, usually accompanies him on space missions. Apart from space rescue work, it is used to service TB5 and as a shuttle for Alan and John as they take it in turns to man the International Rescue earth-orbit satellite.

GrahamBleathman91